Break Free: Disarm, Defeat, and Beat The Narcissist and Psychopath

Escape Toxic Relationships and Emotional Manipulation

by Pamela Kole

Table of Contents

Introduction

My alarm clock was set for 7:00 a.m. and I had worked extremely late the night before. It was not going to be a pleasant morning.

I groggily slapped the alarm clock when it went off and slithered out of bed. My eyes were red from lack of sleep and because I had worn my contact lenses for too long the day before.

I brushed my teeth then went back into the bedroom to get dressed. This was my partner's cue to rise because he also had an early morning.

He was in the bathroom doing his own morning routine and I was just sliding on my work slacks when

I heard him scream, *"WHY DIDN'T YOU PUT THE CAP BACK ON THE TOOTHPASTE TUBE?"*

I wish I could say it was the first time. Far from.

He stomped into the bedroom and stood in front of me holding the toothpaste cap as evidence of my misdeed. Then he proceeded to berate me for always forgetting to cap the toothpaste, even though the last time I could remember doing so was at least six months earlier. And he didn't stop there – he used my forgetfulness to openly wonder how I'd ever graduated from college, how I managed to remember where we lived, and how I functioned on a day-to-day basis.

As usual, he used a tiny, insignificant error on my part and blew it into a diatribe about my overall failure as a human being. If it wasn't about my memory and intelligence, it was about my physical appearance and weight. If it wasn't about those things, it was about my talents (or lack thereof) and my abilities.

You get the idea.

When I mentioned that he, too, had committed the unthinkable crime of leaving the cap off the toothpaste just a few days before, he gave me a thousand excuses and rationalizations for why he was allowed to make such a mistake but I should be crucified for doing the same thing.

Well, I had a bad week at work!

You know that I focus on the big picture of life.

I just misplaced it, you just failed to put it back on.

No, I didn't.

However I argued against his responses, I just couldn't find a way to make them stick and have any sort of impact. He was as untouchable as a Teflon pan.

I was thirty minutes late to work (and a meeting with my manager) and my eyes were so puffy from crying that my manager asked me if I had recently had an allergic reaction to something.

That's just a tiny slice of the life I lived under the thumb of a massive psychopath and narcissist. To him, I was only an object to accomplish a means to an end, no more important or cherished than a screwdriver or a pair of gloves.

To top it off, he's the one who broke up with me after two years of my "not living up to his standards."

By the time I understood his dirty tricks and tactics, it was too late. I had already been hurt, and the way I viewed myself had changed forever. Though it doesn't dictate my actions or thoughts anymore, I'm still healing to this day.

Psychopaths, narcissists, sociopaths, and emotional manipulators live among us. They are never the people you might suspect.

And neither are the people who are abused by them.

If you're in a toxic relationship, I want to give you the courage to leave it. If you're approaching a toxic person, I want to give you an understanding of who and what you're dealing with. If you've had a toxic relationship in the past, I want to help you reflect on it, realize it was not your fault, and find closure.

Above all else, I want this book to ensure that no one has to endure the inhuman treatment I did.

Warmly,
Pam

Chapter 1. Just One Day

Life under the reign of a psychopath, sociopath, narcissist, or an emotional manipulator is a daily struggle. More accurate would be to use the word "regime" because that's exactly what it feels like – like you're living under a dictator who has complete control over you in ways that you don't even realize.

The word "regime" is also fitting because you never feel free. You feel as if you're constantly under a microscope and being scrutinized and criticized; that anything you say is a potential powder keg. If you use even one wrong word, you'll create an explosive situation (that will appear to be your fault) and anger directed at you will be the immediate result.

You'll start walking on eggshells, never daring to raise your voice or show opposition until, eventually, you just won't say much at all to prevent negative reactions being thrown at you. As the other person becomes more and more unpredictable – or predictable only in the sense that you know they'll become angry with you – your comfort zone will shrink and shrink until you're just a silent doormat.

Yes, fine, no problem – doing everything you can to stay safely under their radar and not be noticed or nitpicked.

An exaggeration for some, an understatement for others.

It's an incredibly gradual and unconscious practice rooted in simple psychological conditioning. If you want to avoid these negative consequences, you will stop the act that causes them. In your case, it will be objective boundaries and rights that any person has.

Were you thinking about complaining about the dishes, or even politely inquiring as to how long the dishes have been in the sink?

Think again – that's a question that implies how dirty, disgusting, and lazy they are! Prepare for battle because you will have offended them, put them on the defensive, and caused them to lash out at you.

10

It's going to end with a round of finger-pointing and a confrontation over something that doesn't even matter. And inevitably, this barrage of vitriol will extend to all your other supposed flaws.

And it's all your fault. Again.

That's how it is every moment of every day. There might be some charming moments that remind you of why you are even with this person in the first place, but they are far and few between. They're a thing of the past that you can hardly believe existed at one time.

Most important, they aren't in the relationship for you. Your partner isn't being sweet or charming for *you*; it's for them to feel good, or because being charming at that particular moment serves a purpose for *them*. Your purpose isn't to be a romantic partner – it's to be an ego boost or tool to fulfill a goal of theirs.

Where does this leave you? What kind of a person can remain after months or even years of this kind of treatment and abuse? And yes, it is unequivocally 100% abuse.

The short answer is that it doesn't leave a person.

It leaves a *husk*.

It creates someone who is ruled by fear and thinks the world will treat them poorly because their close relationships have. It creates someone who lives their life, consciously or subconsciously, trying to avoid pain, afraid, and self-protective.

It leaves someone who can't sleep at night because of anxiety and stress – both from staying, and from the thought of leaving. That's the type of paradox living under this type of regime creates. You hate what you have, but you're scared to death of not having it, of the unknown.

It creates the type of person who has a fear or phobia of loud yelling because of the memories it brings back. It creates the type of person who visibly flinches when you reach for their arm because they thought you were reaching for their neck as others have done. The type of person who, out of an instinct to protect themselves, apologizes when they have nothing to apologize for.

If it's beginning to sound a little bit like post-traumatic stress disorder (PTSD), it's because they're not so different.

And let's be clear – it doesn't just have to be your significant other. It can be your parent, your sibling, your friend, or even a co-worker who sits in the cubicle across from you. These dynamics can manifest in any relationship – why?

Because you are a normal human with normal empathy and feelings, where the psychopath, manipulator, and narcissist is not. They don't have normal feelings of shame, so they project that onto their relationships and the people that surround them.

To repeat, these dynamics can appear in any relationship because that's what the narcissist, psychopath, and manipulator brings to them. It's not your fault that you had the bad luck of getting caught in their tornado of shame and guilt. If you have family, friends, or co-workers that you always seem to feel bad or inadequate around, it's probably not anything you're doing. It's an image and contrast that they are creating to put themselves in a better light.

Can they ever truly fall in love? It's not the same definition of love that you or I would use, that's for sure.

Here's what just one day is like under the influence of a psychopath, narcissist, or manipulator's regime.

7:30AM – you accidentally hit the snooze button on your alarm instead of turning it off and awaken your partner. They are extremely grumpy about it, and yell at you sternly not to hit the snooze button, that it's extremely inconsiderate. You apologize, but they aren't satisfied.

8:00AM – you forgot to put the cap back on the tube of toothpaste and you get an earful of sarcastic comments that you can't remember anything and that your brain is shrinking by the day. You note that they've done this as well but, according to them, their action was acceptable (and they will have a lot of reasons for this).

8:15AM – the clothes you picked out for work are criticized, and you are told you look terrible in some clothes and you should stick to the dress code they have chosen for you.

1:30PM – you tell your partner that you made plans with a friend for dinner, and they shamed you for not including them in your planning and say that it was so last minute that they are going to have to eat a microwave dinner alone at home. You cancel your plans dutifully. Your friend is annoyed but not that surprised.

6:00PM – you arrive home to meet your partner after shopping for groceries. You didn't pick up milk and you get scolded for essentially not reading their mind and anticipating their needs. Your partner mentioned nothing about milk. They claim their night is ruined by the lack of milk, and not once do they thank you for the rest of the groceries.

7:15PM – you alone cook dinner and they don't thank you, merely make another pointed remark about the lack of milk.

9:00PM – you've been getting the cold shoulder all night because of your milk gaffe, which you now believe was firmly your fault. You feel racked with guilt that you've apparently ruined your partner's night, so you go to them apologetically, just wanting to resolve this silent treatment. You feel that you have to make the first move because they never have, and probably never will.

11:00PM – you are exhausted from a long day of work, errands, and cooking, and you just want to fall asleep. Your partner starts bugging you for sex, essentially demanding it as an entitled privilege. You give in.

Do you see the pattern? Everything about this exhausting sample day is about pleasing your partner – and both parties act accordingly. Your partner is the focus of two people, and that's not right.

You eventually plan your day around accommodating them and avoiding angry outbursts for "stepping out of line."

What do you get out of constantly walking on eggshells, having to continually placate the other person, and inevitably dealing with anger directed at you? Well, that's a great question.

You're in an invisible prison. You hold the keys to leave any time you want – but you don't.

Maybe that's because the devil you know is better than the devil you don't know. What might be outside those invisible prison bars? You just don't know. Besides, what could someone who messes up as much as you do hope to accomplish or do, anyway?

And that's just one day.

Chapter 2. All About Psychopaths, Narcissists, and Manipulators

In the previous chapter, we had a sneak peek into what it's like to interact with a psychopath, narcissist, or manipulator. Even though the days with any one of these might be relatively similar, and although what I described might have hit too close to home for comfort, these are still three somewhat distinct personalities fueled by different motivations.

The first and most important point is to understand that they are not normal. They do not understand how normal human relationships function, and they are not with you for normal reasons.

A normal relationship might use love and trust as its currency, but a relationship with any **p**sychopath, **n**arcissist, or **m**anipulator (**PNM**) has a wholly different purpose to them. You're doing something for them, they're benefiting from you, and they are using you for something. If they must act a little bit to accomplish that goal and extract what they need from you, that's fine with them.

Love does not conquer all.

They are extraordinary actors and charmers because they know how to use the normal human psyche to get what they want. They might not be able to genuinely feel it, but they can *mimic* the appropriate emotion when they want to get a specific reaction. In normal people, this would be paired with a sense of empathy, a conscience, and crippling guilt, but that's not the case with PNMs.

They lack all those qualities. That unites them all, but let's look at them separately to increase our understanding of who we're dealing with.

They may present themselves with a flawless veneer, but every now and then, between the good moments, you will catch a glimpse of their true selves: blowing up at a waiter or impatiently smashing a wall. This is who they truly are. It's in those instances that you slowly learn that they want to inject chaos, anxiety, and insecurity into your life so you will be more likely to listen to them.

Psychopaths and Sociopaths

For the purposes of this book, they are interchangeable. This might not fit clinical definitions, but it's how people use them in everyday life to describe the people they deal with and the situations they find themselves in.

A psychopath is frightening for many reasons and they are incredibly sharp and intelligent. They're calculating, capable of planning ahead, scheming, and concocting plans that leave most normal people confused.

Psychopaths understand exactly what they're doing to you, themselves, and their other relationships. They have complete self-awareness and know how their actions affect others, what their consequences are, and how they are manipulating you.

The problem is they don't care. They just don't. They might tell you they do, and their words might draw you in time and time again – but look to their actions for a glimpse into their real intentions.

They want what they want, and that's all that matters to them. They have zero conscience and zero shame about accomplishing their goals at the expense of others.

Of course, they are smart, so they realize they need to keep up appearances, otherwise their ruses will no longer work. Social expectations and pressure, and their need for status to accomplish their goals is one of the few things that holds them back from being even more ruthless and devastating than they are. You'll soon begin to realize they possess many masks, all of which hide their true selfish selves. You fell for one of their masks and identities, but don't feel bad — everyone in their life has as well.

Imagine what you would do if you didn't care whom you hurt or how you accomplished your goals? It's a frightening thought experiment that is similar to asking, "What would you do if there were no laws to tell you what was right or wrong?"

Their selfishness rules the day and is their primary motivator. It gives them an impressive manipulative power because they are smart enough to make it appear as if they have your best interests at heart when they are really fulfilling their own goals.

Their utter selfishness results in a total lack of empathy — even though they may understand how you are affected by their actions. You could call them callous to the extreme with a complete lack of remorse and shame.

20

They don't react emotionally in the way you might expect. Externally, they might show some remorse or rue, but internally they are continually scheming about how to extract what they want from every situation. They are pathological liars for this same reason – they have no emotional attachment and just want to accomplish their goal.

If someone were to die, a psychopath might show sadness externally because they know they should to conform to society, but they don't care one lick about the person's death unless it benefits or harms them in a tangible way.

Unsurprisingly, most serial killers can be characterized as psychopaths because their selfish desires override other people's right to live, and they show no remorse over what they've done – other than their remorse at being caught.

Because psychopaths are driven by selfish needs, the relationships they do keep usually fulfill some type of need for them. In other words, they use people constantly, and the people close to them are the most useful to them. They feel no emotional or moral debt to them and will be charming and giving so long as it helps them use the other person more effectively.

That's a very important point to remember – psychopaths are extremely charming because they can persuade and manipulate with the best. They've had to learn how to get what they want.

This means you mean as much as to them as does a screwdriver. You're valuable because you perform a function that pleases them, but once that function no longer matters, or you can no longer perform it, you become worthless to them. You are truly a walking, talking tool for them.

In closer relationships, sometimes the value you bring is purely adoration or love-based. In other words, they keep you around because you give them feelings of validation and attention. To accomplish this goal, they will learn about you so they can better charm you, and they will make you believe that you love them – because your loving them is your value to them.

So ask yourself again, what would you do if you had no conscience?

Narcissists

A narcissist is a person who is completely and overwhelmingly absorbed in themselves. The word comes from Narcissus who, in the Greek myth, fell in love with his reflection in a pond and never moved, thus starving to death.

They are the center of their own universe, and they carry that belief into how they interact with others. They expect others to also treat them as the centers of their universes and act accordingly.

This means that narcissists regard others not dissimilarly to how psychopaths do – as tools to be used to stroke their egos and confirm their own worldview. But there are some differences in what fuels this perspective.

A psychopath uses people because they are missing the guilt and shame component in their brain. A narcissist uses people because behind their mask of egotism and self-importance lies an incredibly fragile sense of self that is tied up in external validation and can't handle any hint of criticism.

In other words, the narcissist goal is to boost their self-esteem and sense of confidence through whatever means possible – and that means controlling or using you in whatever way they can. They do feel occasional shame and guilt, but it's constantly overridden and vetoed by their need to confirm their own grandeur.

All their acts are a result of how poorly and negatively they feel about themselves, though they might not understand that on a conscious level.

The narcissist believes they possess greater intelligence, moral sense, and enlightenment than others. They believe they are special and unique in a way that very few people are. And they expect to be treated as such... all the while hoping that no one sees through their façade to their insecure self.

In a sense, the narcissist is putting up such a sizable front that they never reveal their true self to others. But that's secondary to the narcissist protecting themselves.

They will take advantage of you, manipulate you, and show extreme arrogance – it's an attempt to prove to themselves and others that they are who they believe themselves to be. They are like bullies because they protect themselves through aggression and wielding power over others. If the narcissist must choose between averting a small threat to themselves and inflicting massive pain on you, they will choose the latter without a moment's hesitation.

Narcissists are the ultimate "Me first, me second, you never." To have any other expectation is to invite heartache. You will never be a priority or equal to them. You will never feel in control with them, or as if you matter. You will never feel as if they understand you because they simply don't care to. You will never win because narcissists have been defending themselves for years and are defense mechanism and rationalization experts.

They are like a non-stick pan – nothing you say will stick to them because they will be able to explain it and provide plausible deniability. Eventually you'll feel defeated and as if you are always in the wrong.

Their power comes from the fact that you are a normal person with normal feelings, while they are trying to compensate for one major shortcoming, imaginary or not.

Of course, both the psychopath and narcissist use incredible degrees of emotional manipulation to accomplish their goals. They know exactly how to push your buttons and get what they want without a smidge of shame. It would be impressive if it weren't so malicious. It's how they have essentially manufactured the chemistry between you two, and made you feel you are soulmates. They read you, manipulated you, drew you in, and clipped the collar on.

This chapter provides a short overview of these personality types and once you understand their background, you can work with or against them.

Chapter 3. Their Emotional Manipulation Tactics

Let's examine the tools in their powerful arsenal and how they use them against you. The PNM is many things, but stupid is not one of them. The tactics they use are intentional, whether conscious or subconscious, and are their way of keeping you in line and getting what they want.

Some of them may hit extremely close to home, and you may have heard some of what follows verbatim in the past. It can be scary and triggering.

But let's pull back the curtain and see exactly what they're trying to accomplish and how.

1. Occasional approval.

Occasional approval is exactly what it sounds like. You can do the greatest things in the world for your partner, and they will only occasionally acknowledge it and show approval and affection.

It doesn't matter what you do. They have made a concentrated effort to show you only a certain amount of approval – a quota of sorts – to keep you under their power. They keep you under their thumb to keep you reaching for approval and feeling negatively about yourself.

Many psychological studies show that being positively reinforced on an inconsistent basis is addicting and keeps people coming back. It's the entire basis for **gambling** – if you won every time you pulled the lever on the slot machine, you would have no incentive to keep coming back and trying again. Instead, you stay glued to the machine without even knowing why.

Your partner knows this instinctively and thus doesn't reward your every positive action as they should. It keeps you searching for their approval, which is the equivalent of the jackpot at the slot machine. You may even become **obsessed** with their approval and it may consume you. This is not uncommon, and can drive you to anxiety. Ultimately it makes you afraid of being left by them, so you keep trying harder and harder to win their approval.

It's a cycle that doesn't end easily, and is designed to benefit only your partner and the amount of power they hold over you.

Example: You've cooked your partner dinner from scratch every night of the week. They only really thank, acknowledge, and praise you one of those nights. This makes you think the food on the other nights was inadequate, and so you try harder to cook better to again receive that praise you desire.

Consequence: You enjoy the attention they occasionally give you so much that it's like hitting an oasis in the desert. You may become obsessed with their approval and keep working toward it, creating an incredibly unbalanced relationship.

2. The disguised putdown.

This isn't a book about obvious red flags — there would be no point to that and you probably wouldn't need someone to tell you about them.

This is a book about the sneaky, underhanded, and plain dirty tricks that abusers use against you that you might not otherwise catch!

That's exactly what the disguised putdown is.

A normal putdown is, "Wow, you're really bad at that" to your face. A **disguised** putdown is couched under the pretense of another purpose, making a negative statement "acceptable."

It can be disguised as an innocent question, teaching, advice, helping, or offered solution, but the result is you are put down and insulted by a negative statement.

Your abuser knows that their hold on you depends on how superior they feel and how inferior you feel. They make it a point to demean and put you down at every chance possible to keep this power balance in their favor. Sometimes they are clever about it, such as with the disguised putdown.

This way, it makes it seem as if their **intentions** are positive and caring, despite the consequence of your feeling terrible about yourself. That may be how they justify it to themselves. Your abuser is a master of emotional manipulation and knows just what makes you tick – make no mistake, this is intentionally hurtful. And to make matters worse, it often comes from a place of condescension.

Example: Them: "Hey, you really need to work on your listening skills. You're such a terrible listener. Why don't you check out a book called _____, it's for people like you. You're welcome!"

Consequence: Even though the suggestion appears to be helpful and well-intentioned, you feel insulted and your self-esteem is lowered a notch. Maybe you ARE a bad listener. What else are you bad at? You can be sure they will point it out.

3. Gaslighting.

Unfortunately, gaslighting is a widely-practiced phenomenon that you may have even used from time to time.

Not to the extent that your abuser does, but it can be very easy to fall into gaslighting mode if you're not careful. But that doesn't make it right.

Gaslighting is when you bring an issue up to your abuser, but they immediately **invalidate it** and proclaim that the only problem is with you.

You can see how powerful this might be, as it allows the abuser to deflect all issues about their own actions and shift the focus to something irrelevant. They do briefly acknowledge it, but deflect it all the same.

It's also a strong refusal to accept responsibility in any form, which your abuser prefers because it means the responsibility will fall on you.

When the focus of a problem is shifted back to you, the conversation branches off into all your shortcomings and this decreases your self-esteem. Most important, the focus is never on the abuser and their actions. You'll start to doubt yourself and conform to the new standards they have set for you.

This also conditions you to never show your displeasure or bring up issues you have with your abuser, because you know the result will be an argument, your feeling poorly about yourself, and your walking away with your tail between your legs. Of course, this keeps the power in your abuser's hand because they have just silenced you effectively without having to do anything.

Finally, gaslighting totally invalidates your concerns and can make you doubt whether they are even valid. This can drive you crazy with doubt and anxiety, and make you feel as if your abuser is the only one who will ever accept you.

Example:

You: "Why did you say that to my mother? That was so rude!"

Them: "What are you talking about? I was perfectly polite and you both just took it the wrong way. What's wrong with you two? Don't be so emotional.

You need serious help and you need to learn how to talk to people."

Consequences: After they say that the issue is with you, the focus will be on you and any problems they choose to bring up, e.g., you're being emotional or otherwise in the wrong. This means that the original issue will not be addressed, and you are unjustly on the defensive... even when you are in the right.

4. Setting a smokescreen.

A smokescreen in normal terms is something that acts to conceal the true nature or intent of something else.

In an abuser's arsenal, a **smokescreen** is used to avoid and escape questions that hit too close to home.

Even if your abuser has ultimate power over you, it's likely that you've brought your concerns up to them before. After all, they care about you, right? They should want to remedy the situation and smooth matters over.

That's not their motivation, however.

They may want you to THINK that's what they want, but their end goal is always power and control over you. They know that having to truly answer many of the tough questions you might ask them about their feelings for you would destroy their power over you, so they simply avoid it.

They throw a smokescreen over it and use another issue as a diversion. Sometimes this might just be a topic change or deflection, which directs the original focus of a discussion to a tangent. If you really want to talk about the issue that's bothering you, you'll have to continually bring it up, and we all know it was a big obstacle to bring it up the first time.

A stronger smokescreen and diversion is bringing up a problem they have with you, so also be prepared to see that. This successfully allows the abuser to avoid the issue and continue their negative actions.

Example:

You: "Hey, why do you always ignore me when I say that I don't want to have sex?"

Them: "Sex? Last night, Conan was on and he was talking about that... he had a pretty funny joke about it. Besides, I don't complain when you forget to wash the dishes, now do I?

Consequence: This is a classic smokescreen. They barely address the issue of forcing sex, and the conversation is driven to another topic. Your concern goes unnoticed, and you just feel unheard and ultimately dismissed. The conversation trajectory then becomes their complaint about the dishes, conditioning you not to bring up your concerns for fear of being attacked back.

5. Snide side comments.

Snide side comments can add serious tinder to a flame. Even if your abuser has nothing but positive things to say at the moment, they might sneak in a few snide side comments to completely ruin the positive effect of whatever else they said.

A **snide side comment** undermines the positive content of a statement with a negative, and is disguised as a random thought, observation, musing, or simple wondering.

These comments wear on people when made as frequently as abusers do. Abusers fail to see the positive in praising you, and can't do so without making sure to remind you that you are low-value to them. And again, when you continually hear that you are low-value, it's impossible not to start believing it to some degree. Your **self-esteem will take a nosedive**.

Recall that abusers want to win, and they want power in a relationship. Keeping you in your place with a snide and rude side comment accomplishes just that, but it allows them to hide within positivity. They complimented you, they can't tell you the negative aspects as well? They can't tell it like it is?

It doesn't matter to the abuser how they feel superior to you – just that they do, and a side comment is an easy way to put you down.

Example: Them: "Great job singing that song! You're so great! Now if you could just hold some of those notes …"

Consequence: Perhaps you pride yourself on your singing, but it doesn't matter that the abuser has said something positive. All you can focus on now is the negative comment they made at the end, poorly hidden as an observation. You start to doubt your singing skills, and your abuser has just lowered your self-esteem.

6. The guilt trip.

This is an emotionally manipulative tactic that you're probably familiar with.

Guilt works in the following way – someone wants you to do something and makes it seem as if **you owe them and are obligated to do it**. So you do it, despite not wanting to, and without an actual obligation.

Guilt can operate in many ways in an abusive relationship. If you bring up a concern, they will **play the victim** and guilt you into feeling bad that you said anything to hurt them. If they do something wrong, they will put the blame on you and make you feel guilty for (supposedly) committing a wrong.

If they want you to do something for them, they will make note of all the sacrifices they have made for you, the gestures they have made for you, and any miniscule compliment they have paid you. Your action should be in recognition and repayment of those things. This is ridiculous when you look at it from an outside perspective.

40

Yet all the same, **you cannot refuse**. You tell yourself they care about you so you should do things for them, even if you don't want to or hate to. Out of guilt and obligation, we normal humans do many things, and your abuser is keenly aware of that. They know you do care about them, and they easily take advantage of that ... because that's what they can do when the balance of power in a relationship is incredibly skewed in their favor.

They are taking advantage of a perceived emotional debt in the relationship – a debt that they alone have created.

Clearly, this decreases your self-esteem and truly confuses your mind. You don't want to do this, but because you love them, you should. After all, isn't love sacrifice and being miserable sometimes? Guilt tripping forces you to act the way someone else wants you to.

Example: Them: "I can't believe that you aren't going to pick me up from the airport. I do things for you all the time. I bought you that scone. I fixed that closet door. What's wrong with you that you don't prioritize me?"

Consequence: This makes you feel worthless and ungrateful. By bringing up these unrelated things, your abuser forces you – through guilt – into doing

41

something that you may not want to do or even have time to do. They make themselves your number one priority by making their love contingent upon your compliance.

7. Judgment and shame.

Judgment is something we are all afraid of, but it shouldn't be something that you're afraid of **within** your relationship. After all, isn't the reason this person is with you is because they accept your flaws and think you're a great person despite them? **A relationship is supposed to be almost judgment-free**. But, of course, an abusive relationship doesn't conform to basic standards or common sense.

Judgment in a relationship functions just as it does outside – if you say something to your abuser, they may deem it "stupid," "worthless," or "a waste of time" among other things. It makes you not want to open up to them or tell them anything you have done, for fear they will deem you stupid.

As with many of the tactics in this book, this is a power play that your abuser knows will lower your self-esteem. If they put down everything you like and do, it makes you less enthusiastic about doing those things and distances you from your own interests. And the effect is you **get used to** being persuaded (or dissuaded) by them and shifting your priorities based on their opinions and statements.

Their power over you grows every time they judge what you do and shame you for it, rightfully or not.

Judgment and shame are black and white, and you will be living according to that person's definition of right and wrong.

The shame and judgment aren't confined to the activity or thing itself – the judgement makes you feel personally unacceptable, inadequate, defective, and plain dumb. Your choices are your own, and any partner worth their salt should realize that and respect it and not make you feel worthless about your preferences and choices.

Example:

You: "I really like that girl's dress. It's pretty, isn't it?"

Them: "No it's very ugly and too revealing. She's probably a slut. Do you want to be a slut too by dressing that revealing?"

Consequence: Not only is this a repudiation of a casual comment you made, it's an insult to you. It uses your comment about something outside of you to criticize you personally by directly attacking your character. This shames you and makes you feel bad about yourself, no matter how untrue it is.

8. You missed the point.

This manipulative maneuver is particularly frustrating because it completely sidesteps what happened, and immediately invalidates your concerns.

Missing the point is as follows: your abuser will say something malicious or negative to you and you retaliate or become visibly upset.

Instead of rightfully and gracefully acknowledging your point and hurt feelings, your abuser blames you. It's your lack of understanding that's caused your emotional pain, your misinterpretation and not what your abuser said that is the problem.

Your abuser disclaims all responsibility for your emotional harm, and is essentially able to sidestep any culpability. The discussion then becomes about you, and your shortcomings in reading and interpreting your abuser rather than about your abuser's behavior toward you.

Why can't you just listen better, not be so stupid, and understand better?

This is clearly not the issue at hand... and even if their intentions were pure, does that matter when harm is done? Your abuser will insist they didn't mean to hurt you, but that's often a lie. They know that hurting you keeps your inferiority complex alive and your self-esteem low.

Missing the point is reminiscent of **gaslighting**, except it uses misdirection to attack instead of a direct attack.

Example:

Them: "That was such a stupid thing you said to my boss, I can't believe you said it. I'm going to be so embarrassed by your thoughtlessness."

You: "Your boss laughed and told me he really liked me, what do you mean? I thought he really liked me."

Them: "Oh yeah.... he did. I just meant that you should be careful about what you say. Didn't you hear me? You missed the point. You're so sensitive."

Consequence: Your abuser directly insulted you and avoided the consequences of it by framing it as your issue. They get off scot-free, while you are left wondering whether you are indeed a bad listener, or too sensitive. It causes self-doubt and allows the abuser to say essentially whatever they want, whenever they want.

9. Words of affirmation.

If you haven't noticed by now, abusers take advantage of cycles of love and hate.

They do something to disparage you and make you hate them, but at the same time, there's something that makes you love them and want to stay with them. Often, this love is only misguided insecurity and low self-esteem.

Sometimes, it is a **one-way, non-mutual love** that the abuser creates with words of affirmation.

Words of affirmation are just what you want to hear from your significant other – that they love you, how important you are to them, they are sorry, and how they will never hurt you again. Only thing is – you never hear these things from them unless you are extremely upset and threatening to walk away. Or when they feel the need to exert their power over you in some way. It could be when you've reached your boiling point, but these words of affirmation are what your abuser knows will get you to stop being angry and stay.

Unfortunately, this probably isn't a true feeling of love or respect for you. It's just giving you what you want to hear to calm you down – **that's appeasement, not love**.

Abusers know how to turn the charm on – after all, they are master manipulators of people and know just what to say to make people like or believe them.

Even when you're angry, you are still vulnerable to these sweet words of affirmation, and they completely knock you off your guard so the abuser doesn't have to face any consequences. They make you vulnerable and sentimental, which weakens your resolve about whatever you are upset about.

Just remember, this isn't love. They love dominating and controlling you, not you.

Example:

You: "I've had it! I need to really think about this relationship. Give me some time."

Them: "What are you talking about? I didn't mean any of that and I love you so much. How could you do this to me, no one will ever love you like I do!"

Consequence: There's a lot going on here. Your abuser completely rebuffs your concern and makes it about them as a victim. Your issue goes unnoticed and unaddressed. They break out the big guns with a phrase that you probably yearn to hear, which catches you off guard and makes you vulnerable to sentiment. Finally, it makes you ask if you are even worthy of their love.

10. Altered reality.

Each of our realities are relative based on our personal experiences and memories. You are completely entitled to your interpretation of that reality, and you alone are best equipped to talk about it.

But abusers cannot allow this to happen for two reasons.

First, it would expose all the devious tricks and tactics they use to maintain control over you. This would be devastating to them because you would see that they are intentionally manipulating you and attempting to gain control over you.

Second, it means that the abuser would have to live in the same reality as you, and that would objectively make them terrible people. They might not like seeing this about themselves.

So what do abusers do?

Abusers alter your reality, which makes them appear more favorable to you. It's also a reality where *you* are the screw up, *you* are the person who doesn't understand them, and they are the best thing that will ever happen to you. It's scary if you step back and think about it, but that's the world your abuser prefers to live in.

They alter your reality by making you doubt yourself, denying what they said or did, remembering untrue stories, and invalidating your opinion and memories. It literally distorts your reality to the point where you don't know what's real or not, and you eventually bend to their reality. It breeds self-doubt and can even make you feel as if you're taking crazy pills – but then your abuser assures you that they are right and you are wrong, so what can you do?

Another variation of this is **selectively forgetting promises** and important things... basically, things and events that benefit you and are a hassle or chore to them.

Finally, the altered reality they create includes **direct lying**. Abusers will do anything to get the results they want, and they don't care if there are repercussions for anyone but themselves.

This is all a tactic to get their way – at the expense of your sanity and reality.

Example:

You: "You promised to take me to the opera last week! You promised that we would have great seats and it would be an amazing night out."

Them: "No, I absolutely didn't. You must have misheard me. Are you crazy? Why would I promise that – you know I hate the opera. You completely misunderstood me, I was probably just making a joke. Get it together."

Consequence: You have just been completely dismissed and turned aside. Even though they probably did promise to take you to the opera, it doesn't matter now. That's not the issue – the issue is now your faulty memory, and that's where the discussion and argument will focus. Over time, you begin to question your memory and blindly start believing that your abuser is always correct. This is a dangerous slippery slope.

11. Trivializing.

One of the worst things anyone can do is tell you that your problem isn't really a problem.

It just makes no sense. Of course it's a problem – you feel poorly about it, and it's affecting you. It's like **denying that someone's favorite color is blue** – who are you to tell them that, and how would you even know?

That is exactly what trivializing does.

Your abuser trivializes any problem or issue you have into something small, and essentially tells you that your problem isn't a problem. They tell you you're wrong, your opinion is wrong, and more important, they aren't at fault for anything.

Trivializing is when your abuser takes your mountain and makes it into a molehill. It's incredibly dismissive, disrespectful, and the opposite of empathy. **Empathy** should be a cornerstone in any relationship, even friendship, and the absence of empathy from your partner or friend signals that basic human decency and common sense are missing from your relationship.

What trivializing does is make a problem that you have with them into a problem about you. You're overreacting, they say. You're taking it too seriously and can't take a joke, they say. It's not a big deal. In the grand scheme of it all, who cares anyway?

Your problem is only a problem because you're whining about it. Stop whining.

These are all **cop-out answers** from your abuser and result in one conclusion: they don't have to own up to anything they've done wrong if they can convince you that you are the one who's wrong, or is making a big deal out of nothing. This is manipulation at its finest, and leads to you feeling dramatic, downtrodden, and unworthy of your abuser. Perfect for them – they win on all fronts.

Example:

You: "Why do you keep making fun of me in front of your friends? It's really embarrassing for me, and it makes me feel really stupid."

Them: "What are you talking about? They all love you. You're making a big deal out of nothing. Can't you take a joke? Where's your sense of humor?"

Consequence: As you can see, the fault is piled on you. It doesn't matter that the only thing you did wrong was have feelings of some sort. Your abuser takes zero accountability and responsibility for their actions, and you get left holding the short end of the stick. Your problems go unsolved, and they continue to act negatively.

12. The silent treatment.

The silent treatment is as disrespectful as it is frustrating.

It's **emotional blackmail**.

Back when we were children, one of our best methods of solving arguments was simply to walk away and turn our backs. Unfortunately, some people, namely your abuser, still think this is a valid way to resolve problems.

The silent treatment is when your abuser **refuses to communicate** with you when they perceive you have done something wrong, or when they just want to convey their displeasure. They're almost never correct when they think you've done something wrong; it's a completely arbitrary and subjective standard they live by.

Unfortunately, that's not how you see it. The silent treatment and cold shoulder are a **punishment**, and you don't want to keep being punished and ignored. It's extremely painful to be ignored by someone you think you love, and at some point you stop caring whether you're completely innocent. You just want the pain to end, so you apologize and attempt to make it up to them.

This just plays into their hands.

Like the petulant and angry child who sits in the corner out of anger, so does your abuser to get what they want. You cave because you're bigger than that, and you choose to take the high road. All the while, any semblance of communication is lost, and is in fact discouraged. What kind of communication can you have with a wall? To your abuser, though, it's not about communication – it's about power, control, and they must win.

And because you just want to end the hurtful silence, you acquiesce and give in. What's really being communicated is that you just aren't that important to them, and that you aren't worth their time or love. You feel powerless and betrayed.

There are variations of the silent treatment, for example, when your abuser does something negative and you must comply with their demand to make them stop. You can use your imagination for this one.

Example: Your partner/abuser stops responding to you because they perceive that you slighted them in front of their friends at a party.

Consequence: You can't even talk to them about what they thought the problem was because they won't communicate with you. This frustrates you, and to even begin solving the issue, you must apologize and volunteer responsibility for whatever the slight was. You are in a constant pattern of apologizing and trying to read their mind.

13. You're not perfect, either!

Abusers are some of the biggest **nitpickers** in the world, way bigger than both your overbearing parents combined.

This is because the ultimate goal of their manipulation is **power and control over you**. Even if you're perfect, they will find something to nitpick about you because doing so devalues you and lowers your self-esteem. There's a threshold of self-esteem where you begin viewing your abuser as your savior and the best thing to ever happen to you, and this is their constant aim – to keep you below that threshold.

It's despicable.

Constant nitpicking is designed to destroy your self-esteem and make it so that your mood is always low and you have nothing to feel good about. Abusers turn you into prey, and they're the predator whenever they can be. And a predator can toy with its prey for as long as it wants, and however it wants.

Remember, it's all about control and dominance, a game that shouldn't exist in a relationship.

When your self-esteem is low enough, you'll eventually fear losing your abuser even if they were the one who put you down there.

There's nothing any other partner would find remotely attractive or interesting about you, so you might as well stay in the current situation. You won't be able to do any better.

Example:

You: "Why don't you ever pay attention to me when we're out with your friends? You know I don't like hanging out with them that much, and then you always leave me completely alone when we're out."

Them: "Well what about you? You're not perfect! You always forget my birthday and last year you didn't even get me anything. And I pay for your dinner whenever we go out with my friends, and you never pay me back."

Consequence: Your initial concern is completely sidestepped and deflected. All that matters are your flaws – real or concocted – and completely unrelated to the issue you initially brought up. It's a not-so-subtle way of shifting the focus and nitpicking you about your imperfections. Amazingly, it also manages to trivialize your concern. You are now on the defensive, and they get away free.

14. It wasn't me.

Abusers live in an interesting world. It's as if they're **royalty** in their minds.

Nothing they do has consequences, and they are never responsible for anyone's negative feelings. Furthermore, they are always the hero or victim of a story, and others are always the ones who have wronged or insulted them. They are always justified, rational, and kind to a fault. A modern day **Gatsby**.

Pure fantasy, of course.

This is a mindset that allows a host of behaviors that your abuser can regularly employ because there is no accountability. Most notably, nothing is ever their fault.

If you think it's their fault, it's actually yours. Or you've misinterpreted. Or it's circumstantial. Or it's a third party's fault. Or… it's your fault.

Whatever the consequence or penalty arising from their actions, your abusers will do their damnedest to deny any responsibility. Naturally, the blame has to fall somewhere, and they know that eventually the blame will fall on your shoulders.

This is perfect, because then your abuser can guilt you about something, and twist things around so that it appears their actions are merely consequences of your actions. So not only are you purportedly the cause of the problem, you are vilified. There's no sympathy, empathy, or understanding from your abuser.

They know to take the focus away from them, they must blame and guilt you to the highest degree. And subsequently, all the little failures and arguments in your relationship will become your fault. After all, if they keep saying it, it's got to be true... right?

Example:

You: "Why did you have to be so mean to that waiter? He's just doing his job."

Them: "What do you mean? If he was doing his job I wouldn't have any reason to be mean to him. Besides, if you had asked him properly for the water, there would be no issue. It's not my fault."

Consequence: Even though it is 100% their action, and no one forced them to be mean to the waiter, the abuser disclaims all responsibility and attempts to pawn the blame off on you, the waiter, and circumstances. It's almost devoid of logic.

Chapter 4. The Toxic Relationship Cycle

As you've read, the PNM personality types are harmful and pernicious. So why do people stay once these things are made clear to them?

First, they're not always clear to people that are emotionally invested in a situation. In fact, they are rarely clear.

You only have to look at your own relationship experience to know that this is true. It's incredibly easy to advise and even coach your friends on their relationships because it seems so clear from the outside – devoid of emotional attachment and investment. There is usually a very clear black and white, right or wrong answer.

But when you're in the situation, everything is suddenly different. The small facts matter, and it's a unique situation because of factors X, Y, and Z. You become stuck in shades of gray because you can't see what's actually happening.

Psst – 99% of situations are similar, and because you're too emotionally invested, you are fixating on the small factors that don't make a difference overall. It's exactly the same with emotional abuse and toxic relationships. Everything is weighted differently when it's you, your partner, and your life, and it's a blinding weight.

That's the first reason that otherwise intelligent and informed people stay in abusive relationships. They just aren't aware, or are willfully ignorant and blind to the factors that truly matter in their relationships. The second reason is the focus of this chapter – *the cycle of the abusive, toxic relationship*.

The Abusive Relationship Cycle

It should come as no surprise that there are psychological cycles that anchor us to unhealthy habits, people, and circumstances.

There are three phases in the abusive relationship cycle: (1) Idealize, (2) Devalue, (3) Discard.

Idealize

The Idealize phase is just what it sounds like. As you read, the PNM is in it for themselves. Everything is about elevating themselves or fulfilling a selfish need, so they need to find people who can do it for them or help them do it.

They choose people who are high status or talented in some way because they believe they will reach their goal through them. They are idealizing these partners or friends before even knowing them, and putting them on a pedestal because of the supposed value they will bring to their lives. Of course, this is a fool's errand because anyone who is put on a pedestal becomes unreachable, and the ensuing reality is always disappointing and frustrating. They don't see their target as a person, just a fuzzy concept to use for their own status and progress.

Another way to put it is they see you as a notch on their belt, or a trophy to mount and check off their list. They want that status to transfer to them or speak well of them.

Despite their past experiences and sense that no one is a perfect panacea for their troubles, this is how they approach people. It's the only way they can ever engage with others – they see no other use for people.

Devalue

The Devalue phase comes after the PNM has captured or charmed the target. Reality has set in and the PNM realizes that you are a person with flaws, you aren't perfect, and you probably can't do what they hoped you would. Most important, while you may have had some use to them, it's run out at this point. Your initial capital is all spent.

So they devalue you. First in their mind, then to your face.

They become unsatisfied and annoyed that they are wasting their time with you. They are only keeping you around until they find someone to replace you – someone that can take them to the next phase. They lash out at you, criticize you, insult you, and generally make you feel useless and unworthy.

They become annoyed at your existence and just wish you would disappear. They lose respect and attempt to create distance. Of course, when people attempt to create distance, the typical reaction is more attention and clinging from the other side, which disgusts the PNM even more. The respect and adoration they once held quickly turns to contempt and disgust.

The Devalue phase is also where elements of another cycle, *the domestic violence cycle*, arises.

Tensions build, an incident or outburst occurs, a reconciliation and honeymoon period follows, then a temporary calm period arrives until tensions begin to build again. Rinse and repeat. It's a trap that many people fall prey to because of the promise of the honeymoon periods. It makes people think that everything is okay, and that things *can* be good – but they don't realize the PNM is merely appeasing them, and the good part only comes around 20% of the time. The domestic abuse cycle encourages people to view a relationship through rose-colored lenses and remember only the euphoric honeymoon phases while ignoring the daily realities.

A relationship that is good only 20% of the time is not normal or acceptable.

Discard

The Discard phase comes after the PNM has truly grown bored and tired of their target or prey.

Remember that PNMs engage with people to use them for solely selfish reasons. This means your entire value to a PNM is based on what you can do for them. Once you can't do anything for them what use are you?

When there's no emotional debt or attachment it's amazing how easy PNMs can discard partners and friends.

Did they ever love their targets? No.

Can they really cut things off so coldly? Yes.

That's why it is so easy for them to discard you. No one truly means anything to them, and they feel about you as they might feel about a screwdriver — it serves a purpose. If a screwdriver breaks, you throw it away, and that's what they do to people.

They may toy with you for a while just because they enjoy your adoration and attention, or because they are just bored and entertaining themselves, but they have already made up their minds about you.

Remember they aren't normal — you are. That's unfortunate because while they are free to seek new, exciting targets, you are left crushed. PNMs leave a path of destruction in their wake because by the third phase, they have completely obliterated their target's self-esteem and confidence. The target feels as if they don't deserve any better, and that they can't do any better than the PNM.

They're a husk of their former selves, and being discarded so cavalierly is the final nail in the coffin that breaks their entire sense of self-worth.

What might a PNM think about that? Well, they either won't give it a second thought, or they'll feel such contempt and bitterness toward you that they think you deserve to be treated poorly and feel low.

They'll think they were the victims for being with you.

They couldn't be more wrong.

Chapter 5. Why You?

Throughout the course of your relationship with a PNM, you might have frequently asked "why me?"

That's a very fair question to ask. Why have you gotten yourself into this situation, and what does it say about you?

What could you have done differently? Nothing.

Remember, to a PNM, you are merely a tool to accomplish a goal. For the psychopath, it could be any number of selfish goals. For the narcissist, it is typically tied to providing validation and boosting their ego so they feel better about themselves.

The short answer is it's both your fault and it isn't.

The answer to the question "why me" has two answers.

It's Not You, It's Them

The reason that PNMs have relationships is completely different from yours.

What do you hope to get out of a relationship? If you're like 99% of the population, it's a combination of love, companionship, connection, happiness, joy, laughter, shared moments and experiences, a partner, personal growth, and emotional support.

I'm sure I am leaving many things out, so feel free to fill in the blanks.

But what does a PNM want to get from a relationship?

Validation. Confirmation. Achieving goals. Status. Progress.

Nothing about that is even remotely related to you. Those things are only related to you in the sense that they require you.

A relationship to a PNM is purely one-sided. They just want to extract what they can from it, feel good, and keep you around until they find someone else to do the same thing.

A normal relationship is a partnership that is about mutual love and teamwork. A relationship with a PNM is you unconsciously turning into their cheerleader and supporting them without receiving anything significant in return.

The background of the PNM presents somewhat of a chicken-or-egg scenario. They typically have a history of unhealthy or toxic relationships themselves, neglectful or toxic parents, and elements of abuse and manipulation aimed at them.

Because of that background, they don't understand what a healthy, true relationship looks like. They have never been exposed to it and therefore view their relationships in terms of power exchanges and usefulness.

They can't feel powerful or even secure internally or through their own means, so they need other people to do it for them. That's you.

That's why they want control and power. Remember, the psychopath wants control and power to serve their selfish purposes and make them feel good, while the narcissist wants control and power because to help obscure their extreme insecurity.

You Are Enabling Them

While the way they act in a relationship isn't about you, you are likely enabling them to behave the way they do.

What does this mean? It means that they have made you the victim and your acceptance of that role allows them to increase their hold over you.

You've done nothing wrong, but you've accepted their manipulative treatment. You don't see through their ruses. You don't call them out (or are afraid to) when you see something that is incongruent or flat-out doesn't make sense.

You allowed their behavior to go unchecked by not actively taking a stand against it – and for good reason. Had you stood up to them you would have been punished. Regardless, it's in this environment that they grow and thrive because they see their behavior as acceptable and even encouraged.

But what can you do about it? You know that if you resist, stand up for yourself, and otherwise don't accept their treatment, you'll be punished and even abused. You'll feel tense, confrontational, and unsafe in your own relationship. You'll feel under attack and as if the one person who was supposed to be supporting you is actively fighting you. If you assert yourself, you'll get put deeper into your invisible prison of fear and manipulation.

You're also subject to the two cycles we talked about earlier: the toxic relationship cycle and the domestic violence cycle. What those two cycles have in common is what keeps you frozen – both cycles have amazing phases.

The toxic relationship cycle has the Ideation phase, and the domestic violence cycle has the Reconciliation/Honeymoon phase. We get it into our heads that things are not really so bad because we remember the isolated good times, and they can be very strong and salient.

It's not until a long while later that you realize that you are unhappy the vast majority of the time and simply waiting with a hope that things will change. You accept the status quo (sad, unhappy, and manipulated) because you tell yourself that it is only temporary.

You might not feel it right away, and it might take someone else pointing it out to you, but you will slowly accept everything that is being done to you.

You will even rationalize and make excuses for the PNM to protect your own ego and prevent feelings of shame. You deserved it, and they did what was warranted by anyone in that situation. You're ashamed that you're in this situation, so you distort the story to make it palatable to other people. Sometimes you even believe what you tell others, and it's hard to distinguish how you feel versus how you *say* you feel.

It's all a slippery slope when you're enabling someone because you don't always realize you're doing it. You do it because it's the way of least resistance and to avoid conflict. Little do you know the door that it opens, and that your life will be ruled by manipulation and fear.

So there are two main reasons that you are in the situation you are in. You are not responsible for either. That is important to keep in mind, otherwise it can be tempting to shame and blame yourself for everything.

Chapter 6. Why You Stay (Despite Everything...)

So why do you stay?

Why do you stay despite everything, despite knowing exactly what is going on, and even at times being able to predict what they will do to manipulate you?

Why do you stay with the PNM – as a partner or friend?

What are the invisible forces that keep you there despite your logical understanding that you are being hurt, and that you are engaging in detrimental behavior that will influence you for the rest of your life?

You might think that merely possessing the knowledge in this book will be enough of a wake-up call for most people who deal with PNMs in their lives.

Logically, you know exactly what is going on. But don't think that knowledge itself does the job. If that were the case, consumer advertising wouldn't work on any of us. It's about the invisible emotional ties that bind you in place and paralyze you. At some point, one of your friends might have pulled you aside and asked if you were happy with what they've observed.

You might have lied, or you might have confessed that you are not happy … but it doesn't matter.

You're still there despite everything. Why?

It's because of the way the PNMs manipulative relationship dynamic makes you view yourself. The PNM projects their issues onto you and drains every good feeling you had about yourself to elevate themselves.

Whatever view you had of yourself before you met them, imagine a shadow and a husk of that.

Whatever strengths and talents you imagined yourself possessing before you met them, shatter them all and start over from scratch.

Your confidence and self-esteem will be rock bottom because of the way you've been treated and manipulated. Remember that everything was your fault, you were the cause of everything negative, and it was your shortcomings that created conflict. Of course, you were also the one who started all the arguments, because even though they started yelling first, you *made* them do that.

They were doing you a favor the whole time they were with you. You were so lucky to be able to snag them despite your flawed personality. You were always the one that was reaching out of your league, and they were always the one doing you a service and helping you grow as a person. Whatever accomplishments you've enjoyed, whatever position you've reached in the world outside of your relationship, they are the one who raised you to that point.

When you are told these things over and over, you start to believe them, no matter where you started with your self-confidence. They become your version of reality.

That's why most people in toxic relationships with PNMs are people you would never, ever expect. They might be powerful boardroom figures, but that doesn't influence or affect the power dynamic that exists in the toxic relationship. You'll see CEOs, police officers, and drill sergeants in toxic relationships – and they will be the ones that are cowering with fear and insecurity.

You've been treated so lowly and worthlessly that no one could withstand it, and that's why it can be impossible to leave even if you logically know you can and should.

The PNM in your life started the negative narrative and hammered it home until you believed it entirely.

When you start to feel so low and worthless, you genuinely believe that the PNM is your best option. You believe that no one else will ever love or accept you because that's what they've conditioned you to think – even as a friend, no one will accept you.

Because of that, you fear the thought of being alone because you think it will last forever. You think no one else will fill the gap in your heart that has been pried wide open with manipulation and malicious criticism. You fear that all the insults and criticisms were true and that you truly are a lowly being. And if

84

this is the best you can do, where is there to go?
Nowhere.

You've created a weak projection of yourself so that
you need the PNM – and you've developed a false
dependence on them predicated on the belief that
they are superior to you – because that's what
they've told you.

You also feel guilty for leaving them – for leaving
someone that is actively hurting you – because you
are constantly being called selfish.

Remember the cycles of abuse that we talked about –
the domestic violence cycle and the toxic relationship
cycle. They are cycles because there are occasionally
pleasurable and positive aspects that's what makes
you stay. The PNM can be supremely charming at
times. Remember why you fell for them? That's why
you're still there. They manufactured the soulmate
feeling.

You're hoping for that apparition from the past to re-
appear and stay for a while. For the future to be as
good as you expected and remembered. For the
present to be nothing but an anomaly brought on by
"a bad year at work" and for them to truly transform
and be what they promised in the beginning, for
them to treasure and love you in the selfless way that

you (and most normal people) believe relationships should be founded on.

It won't happen.

Finally, you stay because you're ashamed. You're ashamed that you've let something like this happen, and you can't stand for anyone else to know about it because you believe they'll think you're stupid and weak. You are ashamed of yourself and you anticipate or feel shame from others. It's a lethal combination.

You don't stay because you're a masochist and derive pleasure from your own pain. You stay because you fear that pain.

Chapter 7. Disarming Psychopaths and Sociopaths

This is a chapter dedicated solely to disarming psychopaths and sociopaths, and not PNMs in general. Remember that PNMs, while they might manifest similarly outwardly, are driven by very different motivations.

Let's do a quick recap on what makes psychopaths tick. Psychopaths are motivated by pure self-gain and accomplishing their goals. If they want to achieve something, they will stop at nothing to get it, and this includes manipulating and hurting people to do it. They won't feel remorse or regret while doing it, and can discard people as easily as a broken screwdriver.

Psychopaths don't react to you or your concerns because they don't care about them. They just want to make themselves happy by whatever means possible, and it's okay if that means pushing your head below water so they will have breathing room. It matters not all to them if that means they make you cry, emotionally manipulate you, or rile you up on purpose. They'll get what they want.

Notice the pattern: they control you and get what they want through their handling of your emotions. In other words, they intentionally create specific emotional reactions in you to get what they want. That's their currency and their greatest power over you. They simply do not care about being kind or decent.

If you can manage to react unemotionally, at least externally, that is the key to dealing with and disarming psychopaths and sociopaths. Your emotions are what fuel their power. Without being able to affect your emotions, they will realize you aren't buying their manipulation and become flustered because their tactics are not working. They will be at a loss for what to do.

First, don't outwardly react emotionally.

Stifle your reactions. Practice keeping a poker face. If you need to cry or sob, don't do it in front of them. Once they sense they have found your weakness, they will keep exploiting it, so you can't let them see the effect they've had on you. If they know what pushes your buttons or makes you react, they will note that for later use as well.

In a similar vein, only say or reply with what is necessary. Don't voice opinions or thoughts, just keep your answers as short as possible. The psychopath is depending on you to show a chink in your armor and twist your words in some way. When you say only what is necessary, and as little as possible, you deny them this chance and they will have much less ammunition against you. Of course, their new ammunition will be to say that you are being withholding and silent, but that is easier to rebut than an emotional outburst.

Be as brief as possible and try to keep a stiff upper lip. Remember, you can emote as much as you want when you aren't face-to-face with them.

Second, in your continuing effort to show you are unaffected emotionally by whatever abuse is being slung your way, turn the offensive back on them.

Pick them apart, nitpick *them*, and point out flaws in their presentation or argument. They won't respond well to criticism and will grow frustrated at seeing you appear to be missing their point. You aren't, of course, you're just diverting their attention and deflecting the focus onto them.

It doesn't matter that you aren't really talking about the same thing as they are. If you can frustrate them and get them off their game plan, that's what matters. You can achieve the same effect and disarm them by acting as if what they are saying is nonsense and ignoring it. Being ignored or dismissed in this way will enrage them.

Third, generally focus the conversation on them.

Get them to talk about themselves by asking question after question. Flip everything back to them. Ask how they feel about things and what they want to achieve.

Why do you want to do this?

The psychopath studies and learns about you. That's how they take advantage of your emotions. They're smart enough to know what your buttons are and how to set them off. They need and want to know you inside and out – because that's how they can use you to accomplish their goals.

Never talk about your feelings, inner thoughts, insecurities, and what makes you feel vulnerable. Reveal as little as possible and focus on them.

Talk about shallow topics like the weather, television, and your favorite type of coffee. Make the psychopath feel as if they have nothing to gain from you. They're not going to keep engaging with you if they can't learn anything they can use against you in the future and for their own gain.

They are like detectives trying to compile a case against you. Turn the tables and try to collect and obtain as much information about them as you can and that can possibly be used against them. Psychopaths definitely have dirty skeletons in their closets, things they want to hide – not out of shame, remember they feel no shame – but because of how those secrets might reflect badly on them and interfere with reaching their goals.

Finally, get better at saying "no."

There's no way around it. You simply must get better and more comfortable with confrontation and tension. Part of what allows psychopathic behavior is others allowing their behavior without protest.

Psychopaths are used to getting their way. They don't like being told "no" and probably don't hear it often. In fact, they might not even understand the concept of a boundary or a hard "no." Instead they view everything as flexible and negotiable. To them a "no" is just a minor hurdle they believe they can massage into an "okay, fine." They've done it in the past, so they have learned not to listen to people refusing them.

For example, things you can say:

"We disagree. That's fine. Stop trying to change my subjective opinion. Let's move on."

"It's not okay for you to speak to me this way."

"I won't give in just because you are screaming and yelling at me."

It's a heavy burden but you might have to be the first person to introduce them to the concept of "NO!"

You might have to do it multiple times in multiple ways, but simply adhering to "no" is something you can get in the habit of doing. When a psychopath hears the word "no" enough times, it is likely they will eventually stop pushing and move on, looking for the next weakness. They can be efficient in a cruel and ruthless manner.

Chapter 8. Disarming Narcissists

The previous chapter was all about how to deal with and disarm psychopaths, just a part of the PNM designation.

If you'll recall, psychopaths are driven by their selfish desires and their willingness to callously throw others under the bus to accomplish their goals.

This behavior may manifest outwardly in a similar way to the narcissist, but narcissists are driven by very different things.

The narcissist is driven by a selfish need, but only one.

All they care about, even when being charming and sweet to you, is making themselves feel secure, powerful, and superior. Recall that narcissists are insecure to the point of damage, so they want to control their surroundings and the people around them to compensate for their negative feelings about themselves.

That's why they insult you, that's why they criticize you, and that's why they emotionally manipulate you in dark ways. You exist as a tool to make them feel positive, to validate them, and to laud them.

Any positive feedback you receive from them is to further this feeling.

The first way to disarm and deal with narcissists is to adjust your expectations.

You're only useful to them when you can make them feel good. Keep this in mind, because it should influence how you approach them. If you can tell them something positive or make them feel intelligent and superior to you, even if you are using flattery, that will go a long way in influencing how they treat you.

In other words, if you can tell them how smart they are, they will be subtly conditioned to treat you better because you've given them exactly what they are seeking.

The relationship isn't about support, pleasing them, or sharing. It's about you making them feel good about themselves. Change the goal posts and adjust accordingly.

Second, frame anything you want in terms of how they will benefit from it, and how it will make people like them more. Narcissists just want what they want.

If what you want conflicts directly or indirectly with that, it's going to be an easy choice because they don't want to compromise or humor you. Therefore, you must be able to spin and sell things to them in a way that makes them feel good about it.

Essentially, you must make them feel that it would be a win for them too. You can do this with your needs as well – instead of making it about you, make it about them and how fulfilling or satisfying a need of yours would benefit their life. Stating your needs clearly won't work, and getting angry definitely won't work either.

Once you speak to what benefits them, you're speaking their language and, ironically, putting yourself on their same page. You can even remove yourself from your request and make it about all the ways they will benefit now and in the future. For example, if you want them to accompany you to a family dinner, you can talk about how much your family likes them.

You are stroking their ego, making your needs a clear priority, and presenting them with a win-win situation for them. You avoid having to deal with their inability to understand or care about your needs.

Third, get what you want upfront and don't rely on promises.

Don't give narcissists credit, the benefit of the doubt, or your trust. Why?

Because they will violate it and never come through for you. Once they get what they want, it's on to the next thing, leaving you holding the short end of the stick. It's the ultimate one-sided deal — they will promise you the world in return for something, and once they receive it, they'll go into hiding and, like a shady gambler, never pay.

Most of the time, they will make promises and bargains they don't intend to ever keep. Sometimes, they just forget about upholding their end because they place zero to little priority on you. Whatever the case, do not bargain with a narcissist without getting something immediately in return, and never rely on them to come through for you.

The narcissist sees the world as a series of exchanges. They look out for themselves, so they naturally understand when others do the same.

Fourth, narcissists are driven by the need to obscure their insecurities.

They are deathly afraid of being exposed and that others will confirm their worst fears about themselves.

They have a deep fear of shame. They need to look good in front of others because doing so feeds their self-esteem and ego. They can never be wrong, and they need to be viewed by others as superior.

They might not mind exposing their dark side to one person, you, but if the circle extends beyond you, that's when they start to get uncomfortable and filter their actions and words.

Ask them what other people would think, and allude to the fact that you will be talking to a host of other people about this, including mutual friends and people they know. This will spark some action from them.

They will frantically tell you that you should keep matters private and between the two of you, but that's wrong and unfair. You absolutely have the right to talk with your friends and family about your issues and your life. You are not prohibited from airing your dirty laundry with others as long as you are telling the truth and not presenting a false picture.

They know it's not false, and that's why they want to prohibit you from doing it. They are acutely aware of what they are doing to you, and they worry about the judgment they will receive from others once the truth is out.

In a relationship, the narcissist controls the spin entirely. They control the narrative and what the future holds. But when they lose control of the spin and narrative, they fear their entire world will come crashing down on them, and worse, that others will think them a bad person.

Finally, like the psychopath, narcissists sometimes just want an emotional reaction. They are okay with hurting you if doing so fulfills their purpose.

Don't be outwardly reactive. They are just pushing your buttons and will grow frantic and frustrated when you don't react. Some people might view this as a healthy challenge, but it's not. They're just provoking you versus helping you grow.

And if you ever take the bait, they have you right where they want you.

Chapter 9. Establishing Unbreakable Boundaries

Boundaries.

What are they and how can you get them?

Your lack of personal boundaries is one of the biggest reasons you have found yourself in a relationship with a PNM – if not a relationship, the reason you have more interactions with a PNM than you want.

But as with so much in this book, knowing what your boundaries *should* be is not enough. Logically we understand we shouldn't be taken advantage of, and that we should possess boundaries that prioritize our needs over those of others. So why is it we still end up here, no matter how stringently we try to keep boundaries and even communicate them?

Why do we always seem to either lose the nerve, or become completely convinced that we are in the wrong and should focus on others? Why do we fold in the face of any opposition or threat to our boundaries?

The simple answer is fear. We can't make or stick to our boundaries because of deep-seated, soul-wrenching fears.

What is it we fear so much that we allow other people to walk all over us and have their way?

You fear that you aren't good enough for them. You fear they will leave you if you don't violate your boundaries for them. You fear that you have no leverage or power, so you shouldn't even ask for anything.

You fear they will catch onto the fact that they are better than you, and you have been reaching the entire time. You have a profound fear of rejection. You fear that your worst suspicions about your shortcomings will be uncovered. You fear being alone and abandoned, and not being good enough.

And mostly, you are terribly afraid that if you don't do whatever the PNM asks of you, they will stop loving you.

And that's how your boundaries get repeatedly violated. You'll do anything to prevent those fears from coming true. You place the priority of easing those fears and pleasing someone else over your needs, your self-worth, your rights, and what generally makes you happy.

Paradoxically, we think this willful rejection of our own needs and rights will make us happy. Our desperation to keep that one person happy (or at least keep them from lashing out at us) has taken priority one, two, and three.

The is exactly the mindset the PNM wants you to have. They want to use your sense of guilt and fear against you so they can get what they want, when they want it.

Often, they violate your boundaries just because they are complaining about something or simply feel inconvenienced. When you think about it that way, you're putting other people's complaints and convenience over your needs and rights. That's the logical perspective, anyway.

Establishing boundaries begins with diagnosing yourself and trying to determine where exactly you are too often making exceptions in anticipation of a PNM's wrath.

When do you have the most difficulty saying "no" to them?

What are you doing out of your free will versus the guilt, obligation, fear, or duty they've made you feel?

Are you doing something because you want to do it, because someone has told you to do it, or because you think doing it will mean you can avoid a negative situation?

Are you engaging in the best course of action for you? Or are you actually doing something detrimental?

Are you happy doing it because you enjoy it, or happy because you can avoid bad consequences?

Do you rank your happiness lower than theirs?

Are you afraid of speaking up for yourself because you think you're wrong, or because you want to avoid the PNM's wrath?

If you say "yes" to others asking for your time and energy and you've not filled yourself up first, you are giving from a place of lack—which is a fear-based choice that sours the energy in a relationship and doesn't serve either party. It also breeds codependency and prompts you to attract people and situations that drain you because you aren't honoring your own needs and boundaries.

Boundaries are also destroyed because of an inherent and conditioned discomfort with confrontation. It's inherent because very few people are comfortable operating under tension and anger with people they love.

However, it's conditioned because the PNM has repeatedly lashed out in a way that makes you trained not to stand up for yourself. Unfortunately, part of setting boundaries is becoming comfortable with confrontation and realizing what is happening in the background – the fear-mongering and manipulation.

It's also realizing what will happen when you confront someone over boundaries or about things in general. In a sense, you can think of it as calling the PNM's bluff and simply seeing what happens.

Besides anger, nothing will happen. They won't leave you, they won't reject you, they'll just throw additional emotional manipulation in your direction so they can get their way. And once you start to see this pattern, you will begin to see their bag of tricks before it even comes out. It's all a game to them to accomplish whatever their goals of the moment are; you are an afterthought.

Don't rationalize why you break your boundaries for them. Your situation is not unique. It is exactly as your friends tell you it is, and you are not the exception to the rule. The PNM does not do things by accident, they are not ignorant, they are not innocent, and there is no valid reason for them to violate your boundaries. They do it because want to and they don't care about what you want.

"No" is a complete sentence to respond to a boundary violation. You don't have to provide a reason or justification for why you don't want to do something. If your partner respects you and thinks highly of you, they will accept that answer.

But they don't respect or admire you, so they keep pushing, even though you have already given them your answer.

I advocate creating a list of true boundaries – non-negotiables. Deal breakers. Unacceptables. Essentially, what you will never tolerate or be subject to.

Make sure to create this list while you're away from the PNM and can think with a clear, logical mind and not be emotionally affected or manipulated by them.

These are your ironclad rules for how people can treat you.

Start with not accepting being yelled at, hit, sneered at, insulted, or belittled. It might seem silly to have to get to that point, but start small. These things matter because they set the entire tone for how you are treated. This is your private, personal contract with yourself and you must adhere to it – for accountability and staying on the road to happiness.

Make a list of what you want but are currently sacrificing for others.

Make a list of things you don't enjoy but do anyway.

These two lists are going to be very long, unfortunately. This is part of the realization of how far beyond your boundaries or normal expectations you have been pushed.

Then make a list of things the PNM has sacrificed for you and a list of things they do for you but don't enjoy.

Those two lists are going to be short.

Is that how a relationship or even friendship should be? Ideally all four lists should be relatively equal in length.

Chapter 10. Leaving Your Toxic Relationship

It's been quite a journey, and at some point, after all these realizations and stark looks at the reality of your situation... you just might be ready to leave your toxic relationship.

Of course, it's rarely as easy as just getting up and walking out. That's not easy for even healthy relationships. You're still on the fence because, as we've discussed, the devil you know is better than the devil you don't know.

In other words, you have been beaten into believing that you are lucky to be with the PNM, and no matter how bad your situation is now, it would be worse without them.

But that's living life by just getting by. Here are a set of realizations that you must truly believe and internalize to get to the point where you can feel okay leaving your toxic relationship.

Realize that:

- They won't stop hurting you.
- Change will never come in the way you want.
- They aren't who you think they are.
- They are in fact extremely malicious and manipulative.
- They are amazing liars, to the point where you don't realize they are manipulative.
- They are incapable of having a real, healthy relationship.
- You aren't the exception that will change them.
- Your relationship isn't an exception, and there are no special factors that make it acceptable.
- You have created a story for yourself where the behavior of both parties is perfectly acceptable and understandable and even rational.
- You deserve to be happy.

Why are these points so important to truly realize? Because they signal the end of the denial that has kept you in a toxic relationship.

These are truths. It's your choice if you want to believe them, but it's a very important choice that can either signal a new beginning, or a life in jeopardy.

The next step to leaving your toxic relationship is to start examining the reasons you stay with them, positive and negative. You can think of this as a pros and cons list, but it's a little different.

For example, negative reasons that you stay with them include:

- Fear of rejection
- Learned dependency
- You're scared of not finding someone
- Pain avoidance
- You lack confidence
- You think you deserve them and their treatment
- Your finances are intertwined and you live together

Positive reasons might include:

- They make you feel good occasionally
- They have a fun dog
- They earn a stable income

See what's happening? Soon you also realize that the reasons you're staying with them are all negative and designed to avoid pain, as opposed to increasing your happiness. And if you really think about it, your negative list will be much, much longer than the positive list – because it's a relationship that is sustained by manipulating emotional highs, not happiness itself.

So how do you have that talk with your PNM?

First, don't wing it. Script it like a monologue ahead of time and rehearse it. Make sure you can think about it over a few days. Do this when you're separated from your PNM because you need to be emotionally stable and logical.

Second, what do you talk about? The key here: not much. You don't have to say much because if you do, given your history and proclivities, you will probably start to rationalize and negotiate with yourself to lessen the impact of what you're saying. So, don't say much. Keep it short and sweet and get to the point. Remember that "No" is a complete sentence and so is "We are breaking up."

It's not a discussion, you are *telling* them. The more you talk and try to explain your decision, the more opportunity there is for the PNM to sabotage your attempts and manipulate what you say to their favor. Do your best not to be interrupted and make sure you appear stern and decided.

If the PNM senses any indecision or weakness on your part, they will pounce on it immediately. And you never know, they might be able to convince you otherwise by appealing to your fears or simply acting so hurt that your guilt caves in.

You don't need to elaborate all at once, just say it's over for now – get your closure later or else it will just erupt into a huge argument.

Step three, when do you do it?

After you pack up, after you separate your belongings, and when you are at the point where you are set up in a way that you never have to see them again. We'll go over that part later.

This talk should be the absolute last part of the plan, not the first. After the talk, you should be immediately ready to avoid all contact with the PNM and thus avoid all attempts on their part to reengage and be manipulated back into contact and their good graces.

After all, they have apologized their way into your heart before, and there is a good chance they can do it again. So protect yourself here by planning ahead and making sure that you don't give them that opportunity.

In the same vein, don't tell them where you will be staying, where you will be living, or your plans for the near future.

Step four, make sure to set a time limit on the talk. You can do this by scheduling a car full of friends to come by and pick you up after 30 minutes, for example. This creates public accountability, and you can't very well tell your friends to just wait or go away. Make sure you aren't tempted to remain and be convinced and manipulated.

You're going to be facing a very lonely, tough road after you separate. It's going to be very tempting to go back, or even just send a text to see how they are doing.

This is the biggest mistake you can make, and it happens usually when you're alone.

You need to recruit external help again so you can fill the hole in your heart immediately with friends, activities, hobbies, and family. Second thoughts strike when you're alone and lonely.

Don't be afraid to reach out to your old friends.

You will feel down on yourself and ashamed because of the situation you were in. But absolutely no one will shame you or think worse of you for the situation you were in because it wasn't your fault. People will realize that, and they will just be glad to have you back after being in your invisible prison for so long.

You will miss your PNM, and you will miss the stability and security you felt in the relationship, despite the poor treatment you received. But be aware that you're just missing having a partner, not THEM. That's a big distinction that can be difficult to see at first.

Chapter 11. Loving Yourself Again

What kind of state will you be in after you leave someone who has treated you so poorly?

Unfortunately, the immediate answer is that you will be a shell of your former self. It might not feel that way initially when you can drink in some of your newfound freedom, but you will start to feel different when you have some time for introspection.

You'll be suffering from a significant ripple effect that you won't even realize has affected you.

People that haven't suffered the type of trauma you've suffered will have many expectations; expectations they take for granted. You will not be able to do these things as easily or as automatically.

117

People expect to be accepted, liked, loved, trusted, and treated with respect. These are universal human rights. They are the baseline of a relationship; the starting point.

But that's not instinctively how you will feel about how people will treat you.

Because of how you've been treated in the past, it will be very difficult to believe that people will treat you better than what you've known. And that's the ripple effect – it changes your ingrained beliefs about other people and the kind of treatment you deserve. It's the most difficult part to battle after having been with a PNM, and it can be comparable to post-traumatic stress disorder (PTSD).

PTSD is characterized by lasting trauma, anxiety, and fear brought on by traumatic experiences that persist after the initial experience is over. For example, a war veteran might have a flash of powerful fear and stress after hearing fireworks because they sound like gunshots. That's called a trigger.

Does that seem like a definition that resonates with you?

So be aware that you will need to completely recalibrate many parts of your internal train of thought, and that process can include professional therapy and help to work through those thoughts. There is no stigma around it, and if you feel like you are suffering, professional help is one of the paths you absolutely should seek. If you had a broken arm, you would seek a physical doctor – this is not much different.

Loving yourself again requires a few steps. Expect that it will not be immediate, and there will be trying times. Patience is necessary.

The first step is about forgiving yourself. You must forgive yourself.

That means you cannot blame yourself for what happened. The abuse you endured was not our fault. You did not deserve or cause it.

There is never an excuse for that type of abuse and manipulation. Everyone deserves a baseline amount of respect and dignity. It's not your fault someone else was so damaged that they treated you poorly; it wasn't about you, it was about their discomfort with themselves.

You wish you hadn't acted the way you did, or that you weren't so sensitive, or that you could tolerate more. But that's the wrong way to look at it. You shouldn't have to act in a certain way not to be abused by someone.

It's important to flush the feelings of guilt and shame out of your system for you to keep processing your relationship. If you can't get rid of your guilt and shame, it's entirely possible that you will never move past it.

So give yourself time to grieve for yourself and for the relationship you thought you had. Go ahead and feel sad and angry, and cry yourself to sleep if you need to. Don't bottle anything in the way you had to during that relationship.

This type of outward emotional expression can also help you restore a sense of control and power over your life.

The second step is about finding yourself again, and what you love about yourself.

It's tough to think that you even have any positive qualities after being with a PNM who beats you down regularly. But it's remembering those qualities that will allow you to rise out of your funk and stop being prey to the ripple effect I discussed.

You weren't abused because you were untalented and unattractive, you were abused because someone had inner pain themselves. You must proactively realize your traits and talents to break that line of thinking.

I advocate writing a list to reflect on so you can look at it and remember the type of person you were, are, and can be again. What goes on this list?

- Your talents
- Your greatest triumphs
- Your unique experiences
- Specific times you felt confident
- Specific times you felt happy
- Biggest accomplishments
- What you are better at than most of your friends

List at least 5 items for each prompt. You are an amazing person that is irreplaceable. You just need to remind yourself.

The third step is to reconnect with your ordinary life.

Your life is now a series of moments of freedom interspersed with confusion and fear. It can be difficult to remember what life was like when you were not under constant fear and stress.

While stability looks different for different people, it's universally about finding a rhythm and routine that you can follow in your everyday life.

What did your rhythm and routine look like before the relationship? What hobbies and interests did you give up? Who did you stop seeing and spending time with? Did you stop playing an instrument, or stop going to the gym to satisfy the manipulative needs of your PNM? Do you need to focus on your career again? Did you always want to move to another country or state?

Whether you were physically isolated, or emotionally absent from your friends and family, it's time to reopen those gates. Connect to what you were doing and who you had for support.

You're focusing on the past to help you in the present and the future.

The last step is to start thinking about how you want to approach future friendships and relationships to make sure that this will never happen to you again.

A large part of this will be to think about the boundaries we talked about earlier in the book.

What do you think you deserve, and what will you never tolerate again? You have now had a relationship at one end of the spectrum. Do you know what a healthy relationship looks like? If you don't have that experience to anchor you, at least you now know what you must avoid in the future.

You must actively think about how it is affecting you with new people, and the beliefs you are carrying inside you. There is a normal amount of insecurity, and then there is the amount that comes after a PNM relationship.

When a casual relationship grows closer and turns into something more intimate and vulnerable, you will have to take the next step of informing your partner about your past. It's a part of you that you shouldn't hide, and even though it will make you feel incredibly vulnerable, it's an important piece of your tapestry for them to understand and accept as well.

Explain how low your self-esteem was, and what it felt like to be manipulated.

Your partner's reaction might just tell you everything you need to know about them!

Chapter 12. The No Contact Rule Aftermath

Now that you're well on your way back to reclaiming your vibrancy, you're in a good place.

But what happens when the PNM inevitably reaches out again and wants to reconcile, or just wants to push you around and manipulate you because they can? Remember that no matter how you think you broke it off, they still have a sour taste in their mouth. That's how the PNM operates, so they still want to either exert power over you, or have you validate them in some way.

It's what they've always been after.

You might think that you're fully healed, or fully capable of withstanding them, but you never know. Why test it, anyway?

To keep yourself from relapsing or spiraling back into the situation you were in, you must abide by the No Contact Rule.

The No Contact Rule (NCR) is when you literally disengage completely from the PNM and all remembrances of that toxic relationship. You can think of it as a complete detoxification of what happened so you can fully move on and forget it ever happened. The purpose is to delete everything that might allow you to view the relationship through rose-colored glasses and skew your memories of the PNM so that you think fondly of them.

You want to be able to easily remember all the underhanded tactics they used to make you feel bad, and how well they worked. There will come a time when you shouldn't be affected by it, even if you haven't forgotten any of it.

You are disengaging from them and that relationship physically and mentally, which gives you the power to disengage emotionally. You're taking the focus off the other person and focusing on yourself: something you haven't done for quite a while. In a twist, this is

100% about you and not about them. It's selfish in the best of ways, and you deserve that.

You're overriding the tiny chance that that relationship dynamic can take you over again.

The NCR can feel like a big step because many people feel as if they have to wean themselves off of contact. They feel that going "cold turkey" is impossible, but that's exactly why they need to do it. They need to break the spell of dependency and support from the PNM and find it in other places as soon as possible – the sooner they do this, the sooner they can truly move on and find closure.

You might feel guilt, or remorse because you know the PNM is upset with you. That's okay. You are not responsible for how they feel, and this is something you are doing solely for yourself without taking them into regard. If you can accept that it was never a real relationship, you can assuage some of your guilt.

When I mention that the NCR requires zero contact, I mean it in all forms. Virtual, digital, in-person, vicarious, second-hand, and even third-hand. You don't want to talk to them, text them, see their picture, or even hear about them from mutual friends or acquaintances.

If you do have mutual friends or acquaintances, make sure they aren't acting as mouthpieces for the PNM, and will respect you and not tell the PNM your whereabouts or where to reach you. If they do not respect your wishes, they are not your friends. In fact, you must take note of what you say around particular "friends" because it's likely that some may have chosen the PNM's side over yours. And when that happens, all hope is lost for them because the PNM is apt to launch a smear campaign against you and paint you in the worst light. If they were friends before, and they've listened to the PNM's stories, they won't be your friends anymore.

You must remove or block them from all social media platforms because the PNM will likely try to provoke a response from you through those mediums. Remove all keepsakes, objects, and pictures from your physical surroundings that might trigger a memory.

To buttress the NCR, you can write a list of all the negative things that happened during the relationship. Create a list of 20 experiences, snarky phrases, direct putdowns, questionable actions, and the times you just felt plain bad because of them. Be as specific as possible and describe each situation with at least two to three sentences of context to show why they were so unreasonable and out of hand.

Read this list frequently. Once a day while you are on the NCR would not be too often. This will help keep you on the wagon because you will constantly be reminding yourself of what you are avoiding.

I want to emphasize that the NCR is *not* the silent treatment. The silent treatment is a form of manipulation designed to provoke a response from someone. It is designed to achieve a goal, to get a rise out of the other person, and to break the other person down so that they are the first to break the silence imposed on them. It is a power play.

The NCR bears no resemblance to that. It is simply making yourself your first priority and knowing what you need to move on. The NCR is your decision to recognize that you deserve to find happiness.

The PNM will reach out in many ways, all of them manipulative. They may try to use your mutual friends or acquaintances to relay messages, or they may even find out where you live and leave messages there. In the most persistent of cases, they may even drop by themselves and just wait for you.

When you find yourself in the same location as they are, your course of action is to leave immediately and ignore them completely. Pretend they don't exist, and leave as soon as possible. Do not humor them, and do not hear them out. There is nothing they can say that will erase their wrongs. They are only trying to appease you. Make no mistake, they have not changed.

Always refuse any requests to meet up and talk, even if they seem innocent. Your physical and mental wellbeing come first.

They might bait you, provoke you, and generally make it almost impossible for you not to respond. The more silence you give them, the more desperate and hurtful they will become in trying to get a rise out of you. No matter what, do not reply.

If they are the type of person who is willing to hurt you to get a response, what do you think will happen if you engage in a conversation?

Abide by the NCR and you will heal. It's as simple as that. Don't try to rationalize your way around it – you're an expert rationalizer, but this is for your own good.

Conclusion

So how did I leave that terrible relationship at last?

There was a straw that broke the camel's back that made me realize just the kind of twisted reality I was living in.

It was during the holidays, and we were trying to figure out the schedule for us to visit our respective families. When I asked when we were going to visit my family, he just looked at me and said, "Do you have to? You saw them last year."

What kind of a response was that? The kind that showed absolutely zero empathy and consideration for what I wanted. It was my family and it was the holidays. He knew my family was extremely important to me. Put all those factors together and you get an extreme case of selfishness.

But, I should thank him because it's what finally made me realize what I was dealing with. So dear reader, while I would wish that kind of heartbreak on none, I also hope you come to a breaking point sooner rather than later and start living your life for yourself again.

Warmly,
Pam

66913891R00075

Made in the USA
San Bernardino, CA
17 January 2018